The Amish School

SARA E. FISHER and
RACHEL K. STAHL

People's Place Book No. 6

Good Books

Intercourse, PA 17534

Photograph Credits

THE AMISH SCHOOL
Copyright © 1986, 1997 by Good Books, Intercourse, PA 17534
First published in 1986 (ISBN: 0-934672-17-2)
REVISED EDITION, 1997.
International Standard Book Number: 1-56148-231-5
Library of Congress Catalog Card Number: 84-81142

Library of Congress Cataloging-in-Publication Data
Fisher, Sara E.
     The Amish school / Sara E. Fisher, Rachel K. Stahl.—
Intercourse, PA : Good Books.
     96 p. : ill. ; 22 cm.—(People's place book ; no. 6)
     Bibliography: p. 92-93.
     Includes index.
     1. Amish—Education—United States.   I. Stahl,
Rachel K. II. Title. III. Series.
LC586.A45F57 1997   377'.897'73—dc19   84-81142
                                                      AACR 2 MARC

Table of Contents

Reasons for Amish Schools

Why do the Amish have their own schools? These people want to give their children the instruction they need to earn an honest living and to lead a Christian life.

Amish families came to America several centuries ago to seek the religious liberty denied them in Europe. Because tradition is a sacred trust to them, it is a part of their religion to uphold the ideals of their ancestors. And it is vitally important to them that these principles be maintained in the future.

Is religion taught in Amish schools? Each morning, devotions are held. The Bible is read and the Lord's Prayer repeated in unison. But the Amish want the Bible to be taught and interpreted only in the home and church.

However, as one Amish schoolteacher reflected, religion is taught all day long in the lessons and on the playground: in arithmetic, by accuracy and no cheating; in language, by learning to say what we mean; in history, by humanity; in health, by teaching cleanliness and thriftiness; in geography, by broadening one's understanding of the world; in music, by singing praises to God; on the school grounds, by teaching honesty, respect, sincerity, humility, and the Golden Rule.

The goal of Amish schools is to prepare children for usefulness by preparing them for eternity. The Amish concept of an ideal school is one where children's God-given talents are encouraged to increase and their intelligence developed.

Responsibility and Respect Taught

At school, children are to be further prepared for the Amish way of living and the responsibilities of adulthood, which are instilled at home as well. In both settings they are taught to become a society of useful, God-fearing and law-abiding citizens.

Many Old Order Amish groups choose to have their own schools in order to prepare their children for the Amish way of living—not an aim of the public schools.

Reading, in this writer's view [coauthor Sara E. Fisher], is the most important subject, since it is the foundation of every other school subject. Since English is not the native tongue of Amish children, it takes special effort to teach English word meanings, comprehension, and pronunciation skills. Teachers usually begin by teaching phonics, so that pronunciation is simplified and, when once understood, becomes a lifetime asset for learning new words. Word comprehension, then sentence comprehension, and finally story comprehension are worked at so that pupils can read a story and form a picture of what the story is about.

Enthusiasm for reading means better understanding in arithmetic thought problems, better grades in writing essays, more interest in geography and history, and better spelling. Pupils who learn to read well grow up to be men and women who are able to appreciate good books, understand instructions on a label, and read and understand the Word of God.

It is important to train children to be observant. It is an everyday need, a habit that will help them all through life. They need to be inspired to open their eyes and see what there is to see, to keep an ear ready for the thousands of meaningful sounds breaking around them, to train their noses to identify hundreds of smells.

Competition Is Not Stressed

What goals and assumptions do Amish teachers work with? Some teachers have charts on the schoolroom wall with gold paper stars showing perfect scores. These charts can be an incentive for the child to try harder to have a perfect score. However, while these stars are a way of rewarding intelligence, they are also a way of displaying ignorance. A child who senses that she has been labeled a failure often proceeds to live up to that expectation. At some time or another, children need to learn to work without being rewarded, to learn that achievement in itself is a reward. Competition has its place in the classroom, but too often it is overdone and proves unfair to the less fortunate pupil. A goal each pupil can work for is to make a higher score than he did the day before.

Since written messages are the main means of communication among Amish families, it is important that the school child be taught to have legible handwriting. Due to the lack of telephones in their homes and limited transportation facilities, the Amish rely on the postal system to relay birth announcements, invitations to weddings, quiltings, reunions, barn raisings, and more. Writing legibly is even more important than proper English, since Amish people understand each other's "Dutchified" phrases quite well.

Before children can appreciate arithmetic, they must be taught its value as a workable and necessary skill. After they get out of school, they will use math to count fruit jars or corn shocks, measure baking powder or calf feed, figure how much paint is needed to paint a room, and the amount of fertilizer and seed corn needed for a ten-acre field. They will need to know how to keep farm records, income and expenses, and how to compare food prices in order to shop economically.

Lumbermen, carpenters, and masons need to measure lumber, compute accurately, and give fair estimates. Books must be kept and records filed systematically. Our changing times demand mathematical records in many occupations. Therefore, getting pupils to realize the importance of math in their futures is a major priority for a teacher.

More Differences with Public Schools

One Old Order woman reflected in the Old Order Amish publication *Blackboard Bulletin* about the public school education some of her relatives were receiving. "My nieces and nephews are of average intelligence, yet one of them is in the seventh grade and cannot do simple arithmetic problems without the aid of a calculator. A ninth grader copies word for word from the encyclopedia to make reports and cannot write a book report that's not a paraphrasing of the book jacket. The teachers do not collect or correct even half of the homework assignments.

"Courses range from learning about computers to experimenting with rockets in air chambers. Homework assignments include watching certain TV programs. Then when these young people come to visit my husband and me, they are bored because we don't have anything interesting to do!

"Last summer one niece learned how to bandage a cow's foot, how to help with the feeding in the barn, and how to prepare and can vegetables. By her teacher's comments and class placement, she was in a remedial group because of 'lack of interest.' This year she is taking home economics (sewing and cooking) and plans to go for vocational technical classes in agriculture next year. Hopefully with encouragement and help from parents and teachers, she will get away from copying and calculators and use her mind.

"I have friends whose children attend parochial school, and grade for grade they are further advanced than my relatives who attend public school.

"I think the parochial schools are good, and hope my children can attend one of them and receive their education there."

Group Identity Is Reinforced

Standards of dress are very important to the Amish society, as they immediately declare identity to members of the group as well as to outsiders. Parents are admonished to have their school

Amish dress standards immediately declare identity to members of the group as well as to outsiders. Teachers, along with parents, help children maintain these standards.

children adhere to the accepted standards of dress. Teachers need to see that they are carried out on the school grounds by reminding boys to wear their hats on the playground and keep their shirt collars buttoned in the schoolroom. Older girls are encouraged to wear their coverings to school.

In Lancaster County, one school board has forbidden the use of baseball gloves and hard balls at school. By the children's playing with a sponge ball or other soft ball, and without gloves, baseball does not become a competitive game with worldly methods which might range out of control among teenagers and be carried on into adulthood.

How Amish Schools Came to Be

The Amish felt a need for their own parochial schools in the 1940s after the Great Depression. Compulsory school attendance ages were raised in many states at that time, in an effort to have fewer jobs taken away from older workers by young teenagers fresh out of school. Until then the Amish were happy to have their children attend public schools because most schools had eight grades in one room with one teacher. The schools were within walking distance of the homes, the subjects taught were not contrary to Amish beliefs, and children were exempt from school at age 14. But when children were required to attend school until age 15 (or 16 in some states), the Amish felt that some compromise had to be reached.

Suddenly, parents of 14-year-olds were faced with the decision about what to do with their pupils who had finished eighth grade but had not reached their fifteenth birthday. Sending them to high school meant they had to spend up to an hour on a school bus, riding to a school in town. That was precious time lost from doing their chores on the farm. Then at high school, the children were required to take subjects not needed to prepare them for life on the farm. There were also the constant conflicts of being expected to pledge allegiance to the flag and to use the English language to communicate, and of being a minority. So if attending high school was out of the question for Amish children, what alternative was there?

The Vocational School Solution

Parents started taking preventive measures by keeping their children from starting first grade until age seven. That meant they reached their fifteenth birthday before they were through eighth grade. Another solution was to have the children repeat eighth

After the Great Depression in the 1940s, the law required children to attend school until age 15, even if they had already completed eighth grade. One solution to this dilemma for the Amish was to start their own schools.

In the 1950s, the vocational class came into being. A 14-year-old need only spend three hours per week in school, and then keep a journal of time spent at home learning farming and homemaking from parents.

grade. One-room schools became overcrowded, and the teachers had the added responsibility of providing work for pupils who were bored with school and wished to be free to pursue the pleasures of learning farming and homemaking at home with their parents. Teachers were able to relieve some pressure by making "teacher's helpers" out of those 14-year-olds.

An alternate solution was to secure a work permit issued by the township, which permitted children to work at home after eighth grade.

In some states, parents who tried to keep their children at home after they completed eight grades were sent to jail for refusing to send their children to high school.

Finally in the 1950s, a satisfactory solution was reached when the vocational class came into being. Fourteen-year-olds were then permitted to spend three hours in school per week and required to keep a journal of the time spent at home learning farming and homemaking from their parents.

As the rural population increased and one-room schools were no longer able to accommodate the growing enrollment, consolidated schools were built. Non-Amish children went to the consolidated schools; the Amish children continued going to the one-room schools. This was a workable arrangement as long as the townships provided good teachers and the subjects taught were not contrary to Amish beliefs. But gradually the one-room schools came in need of repair and the public school system was not willing to maintain them. At the same time, the Amish population grew beyond the capacity of the one-room schools presently in existence.

The transition from public to Amish parochial schools was a slow process as the need occurred. As of 1997, only one township in Lancaster County still maintains a school exclusively for the Amish. This school has a two-room building and hires two teachers, each one teaching four grades.

Amish Schools Reflect Amish Values

One Amish girl who changed from a public school to an Amish school at the end of seventh grade expressed the feelings of many Amish parents when she wrote in her diary that in "public school we were under the influence of many worldly things such as television and movies, gym classes where they taught us anything from square dancing to unladylike exercises, and science classes where we learned about evolution. Our parents were unhappy about the silly songs we learned and the load of homework we brought home to do after chores were done" (see pages 44 to 53).

In the one-room school the large family atmosphere, so alive in Amish homes, prevails. Pupils need to learn to concentrate on what they are doing while other classes are in session. But listening in can also be a learning experience. The older children get a review of lessons they had in earlier years and younger children a preview of lessons to come. Older children also learn by helping the little ones with their lessons.

One Example—Fairview School Becomes Amish

This writer [coauthor Sara E. Fisher] was part of the movement of one school from the public system to Amish ownership. Fairview School was built in 1916 on land donated to the public school district by my grandfather. My dad and we five children attended Fairview School. When the township closed one-room schools around 1940 and built a consolidated school, Fairview, because of its good condition, was still maintained as a public grade school. Eventually only Amish children attended, but the school was in operation as a public school until 1975.

In the early 1960s the teacher at Fairview requested to have only the lower four grades instead of all eight. That meant the children from the fifth to eighth grades had to go to the consolidated school. To take care of that problem the Amish built Cherry Lane School on South Cherry Lane, one-half mile west of Fairview School.

Most of the Amish families in the area sent their children to Fairview School for grades 1-4 and to Cherry Lane for grades 5-8. But some families preferred to send their children to an Amish school right away, and by 1975 only 11 children were enrolled at Fairview School.

That's when the public school district decided not to operate the school for so few pupils, and the schoohouse was put up for public sale. The Amish thought they could not afford to buy it, but one businessman in the area was determined not to take the

In one-room schools, pupils need to learn to concentrate on their own work while other classes are in session around them. But "listening in" can also be educational.

The Fairview School operated as a public school until 1975. When the public school district decided to cease operating Fairview, the Amish bought it, and co-author Sara Fisher was asked to teach.

building away from the Amish. It was purchased by the Amish school board for $23,600.

The sale was held August 23rd, and a week later it was time for the school term to open. By Friday evening they still had no teacher. A teacher friend of mine checked with me, then informed her neighbor who was on the school board that she thought I would consider teaching. At eight o'clock that night three men on the school board (the secretary, treasurer, and tax collector) came to ask me if I would teach at Fairview School.

I had a vague interest in teaching. And I had harbored the dream that some day Fairview would be an Amish school and I would be the teacher! I had enjoyed school very much as a pupil and was reluctant to quit when I finished eighth grade. But in those days Amish teachers were very rare. So when this urgent need developed at Fairview I decided if I wanted the experience of being a teacher I had better take it! And my sentiment for the schoolhouse helped me make my decision.

The secretary of the school board explained that I was not making a long-term commitment, but they would like me to try teaching for one term. When I told them I would be willing, the

Children from Fairview had attended fifth through eighth grades at nearby Cherry Lane Amish School (above). When Fairview also became Amish, the children were evenly divided, in all eight grades, between the two schools.

president of the school board arrived almost immediately and handed me the key to the door of Fairview School.

I had three days to become oriented to the job of teaching. The following Monday I sat in classes at Cherry Lane School, which had already begun. Tuesday morning I opened my doors for the 1975-1976 term.

The families in the area were divided between Cherry Lane and Fairview with 23 pupils at Cherry Lane and 24 at Fairview, each school having all eight grades. With the help of the children, and by seeking advice from experienced teachers, I had a good term and went on to teach a second term. During each term there were good days and bad days, but there were many more good days than otherwise!

How The Supreme Court Became Involved

The development of the Amish school system has been a very gradual one, with no clear-cut and uniform evolvement. Enforcement of state school attendance laws has varied even from township to township. In states where the majority of the population has remained rural, such as Kansas, the one-room schools used by the Amish continue to be run by the public school system. In other states, however, such as Nebraska, the age 16 attendance law has been zealously enforced. Consequently, Amish fathers who refused to send their teenagers to high school were fined and imprisoned, and eventually the Amish settlements were driven away so that there are none left in Nebraska today.

The Amish do not believe in going to court to settle human conflict. One of the biblical teachings which they strongly embrace is that of suffering wrong rather than retaliating or going to court (I Corinthians 6:5-8 and I Peter 2:19-21). Amish fathers who felt compelled to shield their children from the worldly influences of high school have quietly suffered repeated fines and even imprisonment for their beliefs.

A Non-Amish Defense Group Forms

In 1967, a Pennsylvania lawyer, William Ball, and a Lutheran pastor from Michigan, William C. Lindholm, became aware of a conflict between school authorities and an Amish family in Iowa. Together with other non-Amish friends and humanitarians they founded the National Committee for Amish Religious Freedom at the University of Chicago. Their purpose? To preserve the religious liberty of the Old Order Amish and related Anabaptist groups.

The Committee got involved in the case of Wisconsin versus Yoder, in which Amish parents were arrested for refusing to send their 14- and 15-year-old children to high school. This was not the

The Amish do not as a rule believe in going to court to settle differences. In 1972, however, the case of Wisconsin vs. Yoder went all the way to the Supreme Court when Amish parents refused to send their 14- and 15-year-old children to public high school. The Court decided in favor of the Amish.

first confrontation between a state and an Amish family. But with the impetus created by the non-Amish Committee for Amish Religious Freedom, the Wisconsin versus Yoder case reached the Supreme Court in 1972. The Court decided in favor of the Amish community.

Why have states prosecuted Amish families over this issue, in some cases even charging them with child neglect and ordering them to surrender their children to the Child Welfare Board? Behind their "official concern" for the proper education of Amish children has been the states' greater concern: their loss of government monies which they receive for each pupil attending high school.

Supreme Court Acknowledges Amish Ways

The Supreme Court decision of 1972 acknowledged the centuries-old traditional way of life of the Amish, their deeply rooted belief and practice of caring for their own, and their self-supporting style of life that needs no higher education to survive. Wrote Chief Justice Warren Burger, "There is nothing to suggest that the Amish qualities of reliability, self-reliance , and dedication to work would fail to find ready markets in today's society. Absent some contrary evidence supporting the state's position, we are unwilling to assume that persons possessing such valuable vocational skills and habits are doomed to become burdens on society should they determine to leave the Amish faith, nor is there any basis in the record to warrant a finding that an additional one or two years of formal school education beyond the eighth grade would serve to eliminate any such problem that might exist.

"Amish objection to formal education beyond the eighth grade is firmly grounded in central religious beliefs. They object to the high school and higher education generally because the values it teaches are in marked variance with Amish values and the Amish way of life. The high school tends to emphasize intellectual and scientific accomplishments, self-distinction, competitiveness, worldly success, and social life with other students. Amish society emphasizes informal learning-through-doing, a life of 'goodness,' rather than a life of intellect; wisdom, rather than technical

Over the years, the Amish have faced persecution from state and local government authorities for their refusal, for various reasons, to send their children to public school. This picture of children running into the fields to avoid being forcibly taken to public school was snapped November 19, 1965, in Iowa.

knowledge; community welfare, rather than competition; and separation, rather than integration with contemporary worldly society."

The Amish community would never have pursued a case to the Supreme Court, but they are deeply grateful for the peace the 1972 decision brought. They were surprised but full of appreciation for the way outsiders verbally expressed those deeply held beliefs which they as a community live but do not often speak. The Supreme Court decision eased the schooling problems for the Amish but did not totally erase them. There are still some states today where the Amish are harassed for their refusal to send their children beyond eighth grade.

The First Day of School

About a week before school starts, the parents come to clean the schoolhouse. It is good preparation for the teacher to be there during that time, because getting acquainted with the parents lays a good foundation for associating the children with their families. And by listening to the parents talk while they are working, the teacher learns what they expect from a teacher.

Studying the record books helps the teacher be prepared for the first day by becoming acquainted with the names and ages of the children and their distribution in the grades. This writer [coauthor Sara E. Fisher] learned that by always having the pupils stand by age in class, one can soon place a name with each face.

In this writer's opinion nothing is quite as thrilling as that first day of school when the children come in eager anticipation of another school term. It is helpful to assign seats on the last day of the previous term so that the children know exactly where to sit. Changes can be made if a desk does not fit a child or if close friends sit together and develop trouble spots because too much whispering takes place. It is convenient to have pupils of the same grade sit next to each other. But it doesn't always work because the children may be different sizes or may not get along with each other.

Ideally the first day of school should be conducted in a relaxed manner (if that is possible with 20 to 30 children who are used to three months of carefree days and a teacher who is too nervous to slow down!).

On that first day there are things that have to be done, things that should be done, and also things to be done if there is time.

First-graders need to adjust to being in school. They can spend a lot of time just watching what goes on in the classroom.

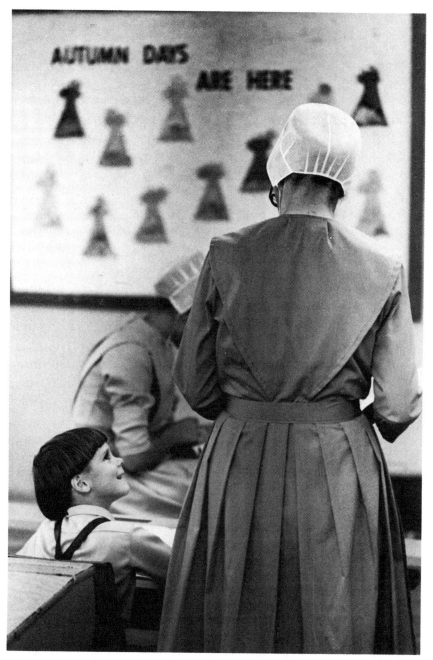

A good head for organization and a great deal of patience are required of a teacher who is responsible for eight grades.

One Teacher and Eight Grades

The first day, like every school day, starts with a period of devotions. This writer found it a good idea to begin the school year by reading a short and familiar scripture like Psalm 1, Psalm 23, or I Corinthians 13. Immediately one needs to establish how one expects the children to respond to directions. While the teacher reads, the children should sit with their hands on top of their desks. Following the reading, they should stand beside their desks with bowed heads and clasped hands and say the Lord's Prayer in unison.

Next comes standing in rows up front to sing a few songs. The first morning it is good to have them go up by grades, starting with the eighth graders so they can be arranged by size. With 30

Singing is usually a part of every school day, whether in the classroom or in the playground.

children it works well to have four rows, two of seven each and two of eight each.

Should the boys be on one side and the girls on the other, or should they be mixed? What works in one school may not work in another. Some groups of children do not object to holding a song book with the opposite sex, while other groups are opposed to the point of hostility. This writer found an agreeable arrangement for 18 boys and 12 girls by putting the girls in the middle of each row and the boys on either side. One must always watch for trouble spots depending on who is standing next to whom. Some are more interested in talking to a good friend than in singing.

The children take turns by the week, two children each week, choosing songs to sing. Usually three songs are sung each morning, and the third one is chosen by the teacher or a volunteer. Two mornings a week German songs are sung from the *Unpartheyisches Gesang-Buch*. Three mornings English songs are selected from songbooks like *Favorite Songs, Selected Songs,* or composition books. These latter books include songs copied by the children from the blackboard which are suggested by the teacher or one of the children as songs they wish to learn.

Following singing on that first day of school comes assigning lessons. Arithmetic is always the first subject of the morning. On the first day review lessons are assigned to avoid a lot of explaining and to get an idea of the work the children are able to do.

Begin with the Oldest Children

It is helpful to write the arithmetic assignments for grades three to eight on the chalkboard so the pupils understand what lesson they are to hand in the next morning. Each morning the teacher posts a new assignment.

Ordinarily arithmetic classes can be completed in the first period, but on the first day that is not likely. They usually need to be extended into the second period. The rest of the second period may be spent introducing another subject like English or spelling.

On the first day, after grades three to eight have had their assignments and explanations, the teacher turns to the second grade. Usually they are given a second-grade level workbook which starts with a review of first-grade work.

Teaching First Graders English

Finally it is time for the teacher to give attention to the first graders. First she calls them to the front of the room and asks them to stand by age. The teacher then holds a conversation with them in the English language, introducing school life to them. The teacher uses the German dialect only as a last resort if a pupil cannot understand English. On the first day the teacher wants to find out how well these beginners can handle the English language and how much they already know about numbers and the alphabet.

Usually the teacher introduces a new letter each day, starting with all the vowels and then the consonants, until the students learn the whole alphabet. First they are taught how to print the letter. They learn the short vowel sound first, and a word in which it is used, such as A-a apple; E-e elephant; I-i Indian, and so on.

ENGLISH, PLEASE!

English, English, that's the language
We must speak each day in school.
If instead we speak in German,
then we disobey our rule.

German speech is fine for home-folks,
All the family's gathered 'round;
But at school we must speak English
So we meet on common ground.

Using English daily helps us
With our reading, writing skills.
So come on! Let's all speak English!
We can if we really will.
—Esther Horst

The teacher also teaches one number each day. There is a rhyme that goes with each number to help students remember how to write them:

For many Old Order Amish, German is their first language. First graders in an Amish school often face the challenge of learning a new language—English—along with their first lessons in reading, writing, and arithmetic.

WRITING NUMBERS

A slanted line, one is fun.
Around and back on a railroad track, two-two-two.
Around a tree and around a tree is three.
Down and over, then down some more, that's four.
Fat old five goes down and around,
Put a flag on top, and see what you've found.
Down to a loop, a six rolls a hoop.
Across the sky and down from heaven,
That is how we make a seven.
We make an S but do not wait,
We climb back up to make an eight.
A loop and a line make nine.
It's easy to make a one and a zero,
Ten is all your fingers, you know.

Only half-day sessions are held during the first week of school. During the second week the seventh and eighth graders are dismissed at noon to go home to help with the farm work.

How Are the Parents Involved?

In the days of one-room public schools Amish parents did not become involved in operating the local school. Teachers were hired by the townships and their ability to teach was not questioned. Children were admonished to respect and obey the teachers.

As Amish teachers became more numerous and parents served terms as school board members, responsible for hiring teachers, the relationship between teachers and parents became more personal. Parents paid more attention to how the school was run and were free to offer advice. (Young, inexperienced teachers were often glad for tips from the parents, but they did not always appreciate the advice.)

Now that the schools are owned and supervised by the families and the church, the parents are highly involved. For example, they take responsibility for the repair and cleaning of the schoolhouse a week or two before school starts each fall. The teacher usually sets the day and notifies the parents. Mothers and fathers alike come, each one taking responsibility for a certain area and all working together until the job is done.

Spontaneous Visits

Parents usually visit school once or twice during the school term, coming without prior knowledge of the teacher or children. In some schools the teacher asks one parent to come each week, making the children feel that their parents are concerned enough about school to visit frequently.

Parents take turns bringing loads of firewood to the school which is stored on the porch, and then brought into the schoolroom as needed for the furnace. Wood is burned at the beginning and end of the season, and coal is used during the coldest months.

Since Amish schools are often owned and supervised by the families and church they serve, parents are highly involved. This includes serving on the school board and visiting school on occasion.

Amish parents are involved in the care of the school building and grounds. They take responsibility for the repair and annual cleaning of the schoolhouse a week or two before school starts each fall.

In the summertime parents take turns each week mowing the grass in the schoolyard with a reel-type mower pulled by a horse or pony.

One of the fathers is appointed to be caretaker, and the teacher reports to him any repair work that needs to be done. Painting or major repair jobs are planned by the caretaker for a day when many parents can help.

Hosting Singings

Parents volunteer to open their homes sometime during the school term to have a School Singing. All the parents and school-children attend this gathering, held once or twice during each term. Singings begin about seven o'clock in the evening. The school children sit in pairs around a long table, the girls on one side and the boys on the other. Each younger boy is assigned to sit with an older one; the girls are paired together in the same way.

Before the evening the teacher and pupils have selected the

songs, planned their order, and practiced them repeatedly. They sing both German and English songs, the children taking turns announcing and leading them. Even the youngest schoolchildren take a turn, with the help of older children if needed. The parents join in the singing which continues for about an hour and a half. Then when the little pupils start to become weary and the older ones get restless, cookies, popcorn, pretzels, and lemonade or iced tea are served. After visiting, the parents finally gather up their children and make their departure.

Surprise Lunches

When this writer [coauthor Sara E. Fisher] was teaching, one family planned a surprise for the schoolchildren by furnishing a hot lunch at their house. I told the children not to bring lunch on that day because I had a surprise for them. When lunchtime came, I told them to get their wraps. I had planned to have the children walk in pairs to this couple's home (even the children of that household did not know about it), but then I was surprised when I looked out the window and saw the father with a two-horse wagon and bales of straw for seats, ready to transport us to their home.

When we got there, we found a long table laden with a delicious hot meal. After eating, we spent a half hour playing at the farm before the father gave us a wagon ride back to school.

At other times, mothers and grandmothers bring a hot meal to school. And on special occasions, they serve ice cream or other treats.

Parents faithfully attend the Christmas programs and the end of the term picnic. In one community a family moved out of the school district to another county, about 80 miles away. That year the parents chartered a bus, and all the students, plus the parents and a few grandparents, traveled to this family's farm and had the picnic there. After the meal the boys and some of the girls went hiking, while the younger children played games and the parents visited. For occasions such as these, the mothers usually plan and share the work of preparing and bringing food.

A Typical
School Day

In the wintertime the teacher tries to arrive at school about an hour before school starts to fire up the stove and have the schoolroom warm and cozy when the children arrive. (It is important to master the art of taking care of a coal or wood furnace!)

Sometimes children bring potatoes wrapped in aluminum foil to roast on the ledge inside the top furnace door. Or they may bring a TV-dinner made from leftovers from their meal the night before, placed in a pie plate that can be heated on the stove for lunch. Some bring soup in a glass jar to put on the grate to heat. Others have sandwiches, hot dogs, or pizza to warm on the stove. All kinds of delicious smells fill the schoolroom as lunchtime nears. (A kettle of water is usually placed on top of the stove as well to provide moisture in the air.)

After taking care of the furnace, the teacher concentrates on the schedule for the day. On the blackboard at the front of the room she writes: "Today is Monday, January 24, 199--." On the calendar on the wall she shades each bygone day with a red marker and outlines the current date in red.

Next, she posts the arithmetic assignments on the board:
Tuesday, January 25
8th grade — p. 377
7th grade — p. 148
6th grade — p. 378: 23-45
She also posts each succeeding grade's assignment.

Then the children start arriving, each one with a cherry "Good morning!" and usually with announcements: "Teacher, Uncle Omar brought us with his pony cart!"; "Teacher, I saw a robin on the way to school"; "Teacher, when we got up this morning there was snow on the floor." (In Pennsylvania German, the same word, *bodda*, is

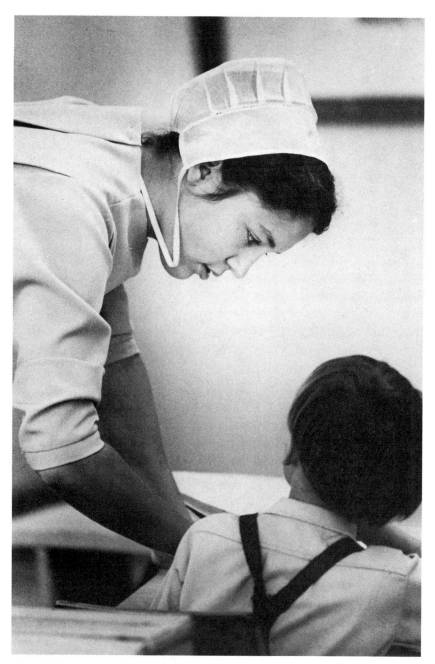

Sometimes an older student may help the teacher by checking work or answering questions for younger ones.

When the bell on top of the schoolhouse rings, the children come inside and go to their seats. The school-day routine often begins with a Scripture reading, followed by the Lord's Prayer and a brief period of group singing.

used for "ground" and "floor," and Amish children often make a literal translation from Pennsylvania German into English.)

Discipline From Start to Finish

At 8:30 it is time to ring the bell above the schoolhouse. The children come in and go to their seats. The teacher taps her desk bell, and that means "Quiet." The teacher scans the room to see if any children are absent and records them in her record book. Then the teacher says, "Good morning, boys and girls!" and the children respond with "Good morning, Sara!"

Next, the teacher reads a portion of Scripture from the Old or New Testament, while the children sit quietly, their hands folded on top of their desks. They then rise and bow their heads to repeat the Lord's Prayer in unison. After the prayer, they file to the front of the schoolroom and stand in their assigned places according to age and size and sing a few songs in German or English.

When the children return to their seats it is time for classes to begin. Grades five to eight exchange their arithmetic papers and check them before handing them in. Grades three and four hand their papers to an older child or the teacher for checking. Then

After the first-graders complete their oral reading, they return to their seats to work in workbooks which correspond to the oral lesson.

grades three to eight start on the next lesson by doing the assignment posted on the chalkboard. Second grade studies their reading lesson while first grade goes to the front for their oral reading.

The children in first grade take turns reading by page or by sentence, whichever the teacher prefers. After class they do seatwork in workbooks that correspond with their oral reading books. The second grade reading class is conducted in the same way. Often they copy a page from their reading lesson for seatwork. After this the third to eighth grades are given explanations of their arithmetic lessons in turn. Within the time allotted for arithmetic, they are given as much help as they need.

Business and Fun at Recess

At 10 o'clock it is time for recess. The teacher encourages the children to go to the toilet, get drinks of water, and sharpen pencils, so they do not need to do these things during class time. But there is time for play.

The little girls may play "Bear." One of them is the bear and tries to catch the others. As they are caught, they become bears until all of them are caught. The sixth and seventh grade boys brag

Both recess and lunch periods provide time for play. Sometimes a teacher must set a timer to keep children from gulping down lunches in three minutes in order to have more playtime.

about their horses and compare their different traits. "What would it be like if you wouldn't be Amish and would have to ride in cars all the time?" they exclaim. "Cars have a terrible smell and make a lot of noise!"

One eighth grade girl describes her 10-week-old baby sister. "There's nothing sweeter than a baby, but they grow out of babyhood so fast. Our baby laughs more all the time when we talk to her. She uses her arms and legs to laugh."

At 10:15 the teacher rings the bell to call the children back to their seats. She taps the desk bell for order. Grades three to eight have reading classes in this period, while first and second grades work at numbers in a few pages of their workbooks. Grades three to eight read their reading lessons and prepare to answer questions to determine their comprehension of what they read. Each class in turn passes to the front and stands in line to read individually and to answer questions by the teacher. In many schools, the children advance to the head of the line by answering the questions correctly. A number system is kept indicating each child's place the next time the class is up front.

Taking Enough Time for Lunch

Eleven-thirty is lunchtime. The teacher dismisses the children by rows to wash their hands, get their lunch boxes, and return to their seats. Next, the children say a prayer in unison, and then remain at their desks to eat lunch. The teacher sets a timer for 10 minutes since some children gulp down their food in three minutes to have more playtime. After eating, the children take turns wiping the desks and sweeping up the crumbs. They may play, then, until 12:30.

Story time follows lunch. After the bell is rung, the teacher sets the timer for 15 minutes, the allotted time for her to read to the children. If they waste time getting to their seats, they know they get less story time, so they are usually prompt.

Afternoon lessons begin with either geography, history, or health. Grades five to eight copy questions from the blackboard into their composition books, then look for the answers in the pages assigned. They write the answers out and study them so they can answer by memory in class. First and second grades have

Different groups of children play different games, but sometimes everyone joins in, even the teacher.

reading again this period, in class or in workbooks.

From two to two-fifteen is last recess. The final period is spent on English lessons two days a week and spelling the other three days. The pupils use workbooks for English but do their lessons on paper so they have more work and so the workbooks can be used year after year. Grammar, proper use of words, the parts of speech, and diagramming sentences are included in the English lessons.

The first day of spelling each week is spent writing sentences to show the meaning of words. Oral spelling is done the second day with the pupils writing each new word five times, in addition to doing the "Working with Words" lesson in the textbook. Spelling ends each week with a test. The teacher pronounces each word for the children to write them in spelling blanks. Then the children exchange their spelling books and check each other's work. The teacher grades the books and gives a seal to each child who earns 100%.

The school day ends at three-thirty when the children go by grades to get their wraps and lunch boxes and return to their seats. When all are ready, the teacher taps the desk bell and they all stand and file outside by rows.

Indoor Recess Activities

On cold winter days children enjoy a dartboard. With it they can play Round the Clock or Stinger. While they wait their turn at the dartboard they set up tables for Checkers, Score Four, Sorry, and Uno. A game at the dartboard might last a few days and narrow down to two players for the final playoff.

A small rubber ball and three clean empty milk containers are needed to play Jack in the Box. Children bring a two-quart, a quart, and a pint size carton. They cut the tops off and put them on a line touching each other. Each player stands at a marked place about three feet away and tries to throw the ball into one of the containers.

The largest carton brings a score of 15 points, the middle one 30, and the smallest one 50. Each player gets only one try on a turn, then goes to the end of the line to await his or her next turn. The player to score 250 points first is the winner.

What Library and Research Materials Do They Use?

With the development of Amish schools came the need for books, reference materials, teachers' guides, and curriculum that were acceptable to the Amish community. Much of the secular school curricula taught evolution, technology, sex education, and other values contrary to Amish beliefs.

In 1948, the Old Order Book Society was formed to find wholesome teaching materials. This group started by soliciting materials that other schools discarded for newer ones. An Old Order Amish man from Pennsylvania bought the printing plates for health and spelling books, and eventually built up an entire eight-grade curriculum. The Amish bought reprint rights to the Strayer-Upton 3-book Series of *Practical Arithmetic*, the Ginn Series of *Learning to Spell*, the Scott-Foresman *Basic Readers* for grades one through four, the Silver-Burdett *Geography Series*, the Laidlaw Brothers *History Series*, and the *Dick and Jane Series*.

Developing Their Own Curriculum

In recent years the Old Order Amish Publishing House, Pathway Publishers, has started its own line of schoolbook publishing since old materials are often outdated: arithmetic books list hourly wages at 75¢ an hour, eggs cost 20¢ a dozen, and history books stop with World War II.

Typically an Amish school uses the *World Book Encyclopedia* for reference. At a recent teachers' meeting in Pennsylvania, however, one of the teachers, who had personally bought a new *World Book* set for her schoolchildren, was concerned about the photos in the books. Many were offensive to parents and teacher alike, so some

Textbook content for Amish schools is restricted to that which is morally wholesome and does not teach about God. Such teaching is considered sacred and is reserved for home and church.

of the parents proposed cutting out the pages with objectionable photos. To avoid destroying the costly reference books, the school board and the teacher compromised and decided to use a black felt tip marker to black out offensive pictures.

While the content of textbooks is restricted to those that are morally wholesome and those that do not teach about God (since that is considered sacred and should be done in the home and church), Amish children usually have access to a broad scope of reading material. Favorites are *Heidi* by Johanna Spyri, *Little Women* by Louisa May Alcott, the Laura Ingalls Wilder books and others. Fairy tales or mythical fiction such as the Narnia tales by C. S. Lewis are, however, usually not used.

Tips for Teachers Available

Most Amish schools offer a cupboard or shelf of library books for reference or for the children to enjoy when they have finished their lessons and are waiting for their turn to recite or talk to the teacher.

Pathway Publishers developed *Blackboard Bulletin*, a monthly magazine for teachers, 27 years ago. Begun originally as a circle letter with six teachers participating, the *Bulletin* regularly carries tips on teaching and advice about how to handle teaching difficulties and discipline problems.

In a recent issue of *Blackboard Bulletin,* one teacher asked in the "Opinions, Please!" column, "What would you do if a car stopped at your farm and asked to see what an Amish house or barn looks like? You'd probably show it to them. But what if this happened every other day? So far private farms are safe from such a problem, but some Amish schools aren't."

Nine teachers responded with comments such as:

"Most times tourists seem a nuisance to me, but I guess if I were traveling for pleasure I would like to travel slowly and ask a lot of questions, too. I do not like it when they take pictures of the children, and I often ask or motion for them to move on. Some do, but others are determined to have a picture. I try not to allow the children to call out 'No pictures' or to make faces, nor are they to run out to the fence when a car stops. But it seems that it is hard

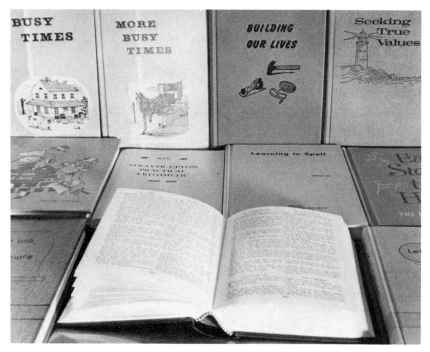

The Old Order Book Society in Lancaster County, Pennsylvania, reprints textbooks discarded by public schools for newer material, but still considered wholesome by the Amish. Pathway, the Old Order publisher in Aylmer, Ontario, prints textbooks especially for Amish schools.

for the little ones just to keep on playing." Another said, "I do not feel that tourists and Amish parochial schools make a very good combination, mainly because of the tremendous exploitation of the Amish by the outside world today. I feel that I would be helping along with this if I encouraged tourists to visit our school.

"There have been times when one or two stopped and asked to see the schoolroom. If this was after school hours I let them observe the room. I do not feel that we should be rude or disrespectful toward them. This would be defeating our purpose."

Diary of an Amish Schoolgirl

March 5th, Wed.

Dear Diary, I have exciting news—there is to be a meeting this evening at our neighbor's place to discuss the building of a parochial school in this area. For some time now, Dad and Mother have been concerned about my brother and sisters and I going tot he local public school, where we are under the influence of so many worldly things. Such as T.V. and movies, and gym classes where we are taught anything from square dancing to unladylike exercises, and the science classes where we are taught evolution. They also aren't too happy about the silly songs we learn and the load of homework we drag home, but barely have time to do after we've done all our chores. There are so many things that they as Amish parents don't like to see their children exposed to, and I'm really wondering if our dream of an Amish school will finally become a reality?!?

April 3rd, Thurs.

Well, they have really decided to build a new school! And even more thrilling, they have decided to build it in our meadow, right across the road from us! It is hard to imagine going to a one-room school, much less to one built on our property. They have also elected a school board now, a president, secretary, treasurer, and also a tax collector. Dad has been elected as a treasurer, which means he is supposed to keep track of the money, which they collect as taxes from each Amish family in the neighborhood, and those with scholars pay so much more per pupil. Dad doesn't get a salary, and neither does Mother, whose job is to go with the other board members' wives to buy school books and supplies.

May 5th, Mon.

The surveyor came today to mark off the boundaries for the schoolyard. They have dug a foundation and are busy laying the concrete blocks whenever someone has time to come and help. I can usually hardly wait to come home from school to see how much progress they have made.

June 6th, Fri.

Well, school is over for this year and it seems strange to think I'll never again ride on a school bus or go to a public school, although I'm really looking forward to the change. Progress on the schoolhouse is rapid, the rafters came now and the roof is going on. They are looking for a teacher . . .

July 19th, Sat.

The building across the road looks more and more like a real schoolhouse—it has windows and doors now. Dad is busy plastering the interior of it now. They hired a teacher now, a middle-aged non-Amish lady. Usually our schools have Amish teachers, but since none were available, they were just glad to learn of this Catholic woman who is willing to teach. She stopped by not too long ago and I think we shall like her as a teacher.

Aug. 1st. Fri.

I helped a lot of other girls from this neighborhood paint the long board fence that surrounds our schoolyard. We had a lot of fun working together and talking and laughing as we painted. I'm finding out that it certainly takes a lot of hard work to build a new school, but with everyone pitching in and doing their share, the work is slowly but surely getting done. The men are busy measuring and hammering and sawing while the women sand and paint and varnish, and we do whatever we can, whether it is picking up rocks from the schoolyard or painting fence. What a busy, exciting summer this is!

Sept. 2nd. Tues.

Today was the never-to-be-forgotten day that our brand-new school building opened its doors as a real school. Somehow it was completed on time. Everything looks and smells so clean and new. It certainly seems different from a public school because you know all the people (as they're your neighbors) and because we have all the grades in one room. We have 40 pupils, from grades 1 to 8, and in my class there are 5 girls and 1 boy. Sometimes it is a little difficult to concentrate on my lessons when other grades are having classes-especially those cute little firstgraders!-but I'm sure we'll soon adjust.

Oct. 2nd, Thurs.

It's hard to believe that I've gone to this school a whole month now-how little time it has taken to get used to all the changes! I'm sure I would never want to go back to the public school. This school is much more like a big casual sort of family. We have now learned to concentrate better when other grades are having their classes, but I'm sure it takes a lot of good management on the teacher's part to keep all these grades busy. (We also have devotions every morning-also singing, for which we all stand in the front of the room.) She posted a schedule now. We all have arithmetic every day except Friday, also spelling and phonics. Monday and Tuesdays we have History and/or Geography, Wednesday afternoon we have German (someone comes in to teach it as we have a non-Amish teacher), Thursdays we have reading, and Fridays we have health and special activities-art, spelling bees, or games.

Nov. 5th, Wed.

It certainly is fun to take classes, as I've been doing these last days when teacher is rushed for time. I'm sure it's

an educational experience as well. I also think that a one-room school has its advantages in other ways, even though we don't have all the learning materials we had out at the other school. (We do have an encyclopedia, a small library, wall maps, etc.) One thing I noticed is that the younger grades can learn a lot by listening to the upper grades, as evidenced by the questions that my little brother sometimes asks, concerning things he heard us read or discuss. It is also an advantage that we older ones are on hand to help our younger siblings if they have a problem or hurt themselves. For instance, yesterday I came over with my little brother when he fell and scraped open his knee, and doctored it up for him. This evening we had the monthly board meeting here—the school board members take turns having it in their home. They go over the books, discuss problems, and it is also then that the teacher can make any special requests, etc.

Dec. 1st, Mom.

We are learning how to take care of the big coal stove that sits up front in the corner and heats the schoolhouse, but for some reason the fire went out

this morning and we had a cold schoolroom. We were around with our coats on all morning until we finally got the balky stove roaring. When the teacher saw how cold the little ones hands were, she had them come up and stand around the stove (they looked like chicks clustered around their mother hen!) and they were counting and saying their alphabet. By the afternoon, when the stove really got going and the sun shone in, it almost reached the melting point in there! The boys take turns carrying coal and taking ashes out, and also help us sweep or mop the schoolhouse. Us girls are usually responsible for the dusting, watering the plants, etc. At first it seemed rather strange to have to keep the schoolhouse clean ourselves, but I'm sure it's a good experience for us in learning to work together.

We are getting excited about putting on a Christmas program, and are practicing our songs, poems, and parts for the plays and skits. We also drew names and will exchange our gifts at the Christmas party after the program. It's fun to try to guess who has my name.

Jan. 2nd, Friday

Now a new year has begun and Christmas is all over for another whole

year. We were taking down the
Christmas decorations today, and we also
took down the old drapes that served as
curtains for our Christmas program. All
the parents were here and seemed to
enjoy the entertainment. Afterwards we
exchanged our gifts and had
refreshments.

Some of the boys brought their sleds
along, and we are having fun in the
snow with those, and also making fox and
geese trails, and sometimes, of course, we
have snow battles!

Feb. 13, Friday

We exchanged our valentines, and also
had our valentine party. We were told to
each fix a lunch and then we drew
names and exchanged them. I had mine
decorated with lace and hearts (and was
quite relieved that I didn't have a boy's
name!). Someone made their lunch so
that it had a false bottom, another had
theirs fixed to look like a bird-feeder.

Feb. 13, Friday

We are still having snow sometimes
and when the teacher can't come, one of
the parents substitutes. It seemed funny
to have Dad as a teacher one day!

March 3, Tues.

Even though we can't play outside, we still have plenty to do inside. We play games like Monopoly, Sorry, etc., and work on the scrapbook we are making for a shut-in, or work on the projects we have started. We made pincushions with canning rings and lids and stuffed toys out of felt. One afternoon when it wasn't quite so cold we went for a walk up the road to go and sing for an old lady, which was fun. I worked on a book report about The Robe today.

April 27th, Mon.

Today we took a school trip and went to visit a neighboring school. They sang for us, and we watched them have a few classes, and then we had a friendly game of baseball. Since it is warmer outside, we play baseball and really have exciting games. One other mild day we went for a hike in a nearby forest, and had a sort of informal nature lesson, which we all enjoyed.

May 22nd, Friday

It is hard to believe that this whole school year is gone already and this was the last day of school. We went for our

report cards and were there for several hours, and had fun with the pets that people brought to school. We had quite a variety, ponies, dogs, and kittens, chicks and even a few rabbits.

Yesterday we had the school picnic-it was such a beautiful day for it, and we had a lot of people here, with the parents and younger brothers and sisters. Everyone brought something along to eat and after lunch, the teacher and the president each made a speech, and then us eighth graders were asked to come up front and we were given our graduation gifts-a plate with our name, date, and school name on it. After that, we played a game of baseball, scholars vs. the fathers and it certainly was fun to watch them-they may be a little rusty with their catching, but they sure are terrific hitters, and even managed to win the game!

It certainly is hard to believe that I am through school now, all except for Vocational School, which I'll attend a half day a week until I am 14.

I will miss school, but am very grateful that I had a chance to attend a parochial school.

—Adapted from the diary of an anonymous Amish school girl. Used by permission.

How Are Amish Schools Supervised?

School boards oversee Amish schools and are responsible for hiring teachers, providing the schools with needed supplies, collecting school taxes, and acting as consultants to parents and teachers. In some districts each school has its own board of three members, while in other districts a five-member board oversees two or three schools.

In Lancaster County a five-member board has a president, secretary, treasurer, and two tax collectors. On a three-member board the treasurer collects the taxes. A term may be either three or five years depending on the number of men on the board. (Women do not serve on school boards). The expiration of terms are staggered so that a new member is voted in each year.

At an annual meeting parents of the schoolchildren in the district select candidates from within their group as nominees for membership on the school board.

Regular board meetings are held once a month and are attended by board members and teachers. On those occasions the teachers receive their monthly salaries. In the district where this writer [coauthor Sara E. Fisher] taught, the board met at one of the three schools under its supervision on the first Monday of each month. School was dismissed at 2 p.m. at the school where the meeting was to be held, and the board members and the other two teachers could come early to visit classes. Before dismissal the schoolchildren always sang a few songs for the guests.

Some districts have board meetings in the homes of board members or parents and are attended by parents as well as board members and teachers.

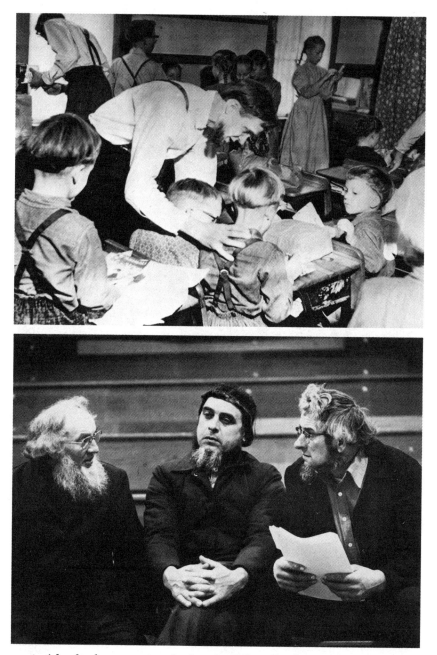

Amish schools are overseen by boards of from three to five men (women do not serve on the school board). The board hires teachers, provides supplies, collects school taxes, and serves as a consultant for teachers and parents.

School board meetings, usually held once a month, are attended by board members and teachers. Meetings may be held at the school or at the home of a board member.

The school board collects taxes from Amish school parents and from property-owning church members to meet the expenses of running their school. Some expenses are physically met by the persons involved!

What Happens at Board Meetings?

At board meetings business matters are transacted, teachers present needs for supplies, and any problem that occurred is brought to the attention of the school board.

The teacher's salary is established by each district separately and varies according to the need for transporation or room and board if the teacher does not live with her or his parents.

School taxes are collection from all Amish school parents, church members, and property owners. The amount of tax paid by each member is partly based on the state's property assesments. Building expenses and special education costs are funded by donations and collections as needed.

In one small Amish community where there are only three schools, funding is done on a freewill offering basis. There is no tuition or school tax. Parents are informed about expenses so that each family has some idea of their share, but they give according to what they can afford.

Teachers' Meetings

The majority of Amish teachers are young, single women. Married men may teach but seldom married women, who usually start their families shortly after marriage.

Most Amish schools hire teachers of their own faith. In Pennsylvania some Amish schools have conservative Mennonite teachers, since sometimes these schools are run cooperatively by the Old Order Amish and Old Order Mennonites. In Kansas, where the Amish attend public rural one-room schools, the teachers are hired by the state and are usually non-Amish but are sympathetic to their way of life. Most non-Amish teachers with college degrees would not choose a school operated by the Amish since their pay scale does not match that of a public school system. Teaching, for an Amish teacher, is a labor of love and dedication and is considered a sacred service for which money cannot be the incentive.

How Amish Teachers Are Trained

In the past, many states have tried to insist that teachers for the Amish schools have a college degree. They did not specify whether that degree was in elementary education or in computer technology or in marine biology. The Amish community has steadfastly refused to send their teachers for higher education beyond eighth grade. They see danger in that exposure for their teachers. Furthermore they prefer to emphasize practical learning rather than "book knowledge." Some Amish teachers have on occasion started taking college courses by correspondence, but in every case known to this writer [coauthor Sara E. Fisher], they dropped their courses after a conversation with the church leadership.

The Amish community has developed a whole network of support and training for its new teachers. In Pennsylvania teachers get together five times during each school year for a special meeting designed to help, inspire, and encourage new

Most Amish teachers are young, single women. Married men may teach but seldom married women, who usually start their own families shortly after marriage.

The Amish emphasize practical learning rather than "book knowledge." For that reason, they do not find it necessary for teachers to have formal training or more than an eighth grade education.

teachers. Four of the older and more experienced teachers are on the committee to plan these meetings. Teachers all over the county dismiss their classes early that day and arrive in vans and cars with hired drivers to whichever school is hosting the event.

Questions and Demonstrations Fill the Afternoon

Up to 120 persons crowd into the schoolhouse and sit on benches and at the children's school desks. The first-time, less experienced teachers have the seats of honor around a table set up in the middle of the room.

The meeting begins about 2:30 in the afternoon with singing and prayer. A program (run off on school duplicating machines) lists new songs, poems, and spelling and arithmetic tests. Older teachers take turns at the blackboard showing methods to teach multiplication, ideas on how to keep children occupied, and new

German vocabulary. The new teachers are given the first chance at taking turns in responding to problems. Some former teachers, parents, and school board members attend also.

After a supper of packed sandwiches comes a special time of questions and answers. All teachers have had the chance to write a problem on a piece of paper (without signature) and have put it into a box which has circulated around the room. Older, more experienced teachers and some board members are given the questions to read aloud and then answer to the best of their knowledge. Typical questions deal with discipline problems, how to help a child stop daydreaming and concentrate, and the availability of teaching materials. After the assigned teacher has answered, the question is opened up for anyone else to contribute. Frequently the teachers who originally asked the questions will identify themselves to clarify their questions, or they may remain silent. Answers reflect experiences, not speculation or

An Amish teacher considers teaching a labor of love for and dedication to young people—a sacred service for which money cannot be the incentive.

psychological training. The meeting dismisses around 8 o'clock in the evening after additional songs and prayer.

Amish Magazine—A Forum for Teachers

The *Blackboard Bulletin,* a monthly periodical primarily for Amish teachers, gives substantial space to questions from teachers. It also invites responses and regularly prints them, thereby making possible the airing of problems and the sharing of wisdom.

Following is a suggestion that appeared in the "Letters" column:

"I've often found that one problem we Amish have is in knowing how to pronounce English words. Many English words are not pronounced the way they look. There is also the problem of knowing where to put the accent. Part of the reason for this is because much of our contact with the outside world is reading rather than radio and television, so we don't hear words pronounced correctly. If we go to school where an Amish teacher is teaching English, but perhaps doesn't pronounce the words correctly either, how are we supposed to learn better? Few people have the time to look up every word in the dictionary before pronouncing it!

"Many times I have been embarrassed upon finding that for years I have been saying a word wrong and didn't even know it. Of

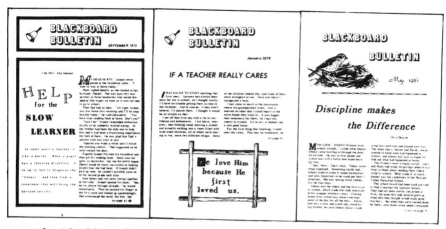

The Blackboard Bulletin, *a monthly magazine for teachers, carries tips about teaching and handling teaching difficulties and discipline problems.* The Bulletin *regularly gives space to questions from teachers and invites responses.*

course, this isn't the worst thing in the world, but, on the other hand, it doesn't give the best impression of our level of education in our Amish schools if we don't even know how to pronounce some fairly common words like 'discipline.'

"I have thought that it might be helpful for many of us if someone drew up a list of the most frequently mispronounced words among us Amish, and showed with accents and spelling what the correct pronunciation is. I wondered if you would put a notice in the *Bulletin*, asking teachers and others to send in a list of the words they have mispronounced themselves, or words that they hear others mispronounce. Maybe from the help given, a list could then be drawn up that would be helpful in every community.

—Still learning, Ontario."

"(Editor's note: We are agreed that such a list would be helpful, and hope the readers will help by sending in words that were or still are difficult for them. We will be glad to hear from you, whether you have three words to add to the list, or three dozen.)"

How Grading Is Handled

The report cards used in Lancaster County, Pennsylvania, Amish schools shows this relationship between percentages and letters: 100% is A+, 93-99% is A, 86-92% is B, 77-85% is C, 70-76% is D, 69% and below is F. 70% is passing.

Arithmetic, English, and spelling are graded by percentages. Daily scores are recorded if possible and are averaged for report card markings. Subjects like health, history, and geography are graded according to marks achieved on tests. Reading, German, and penmanship are judged by ability and neatness.

In some schools a point system is used for marking deportment. Points are added for good conduct and subtracted for misbehavior, thereby arriving at a letter to record on the report card.

The report cards have a detailed section for marking behavioral patterns so that if a low mark is shown in deportment, the teacher can show the reason by checking the appropriate section: "Whispers too much," "Inclined to mischief," or "Annoys others." The report cards are printed both by a Lancaster, Pennsylvania, Amish publisher and by Rod and Staff Publishers, Crockett, Kentucky. Report cards are marked and sent home for the parents to sign at the end of each six-week period. There are six periods in a school term of 180 days.

Charts Give Incentive

In addition to report cards, some teachers display charts on their walls to give children the incentive to earn rewards. For pupils in the lower grades a rabbit hops forward every time a point is earned. After a certain number of points are totalled, a star is added to the chart bearing each pupil's name. In the upper grades, pupils may be represented by clocks on which the hand is moved to the next number each time a point is earned.

Amish children receive regular report cards. They are graded on academic subjects, such as arithmetic and geography, and are also evaluated on behavior, or "deportment."

Some Amish teachers provide incentive for hard work by posting charts that show the children's progress or by designating a special place to display good work for the whole school to see.

Each time the hand reaches 12 a seal is added to a chart or another reward is given.

Special Times and Holidays

Most Amish schools take very few holidays. Instead they prefer to fill their quota of required school days and then take an extended summer vacation, when children are needed most on the farm to help with the planting and harvesting.

A few occasions, however, call for celebration. Recently a majority of Amish schools have begun giving special Christmas programs for parents, relatives, and friends. The school board and church leadership do not want the focus of Christmas to be lost. That means excluding songs, poems, and plays that deal with Santa Claus and the Christmas tree from programs. Some Amish schools discourage any skits or plays, but encourage children to sing and recite by memory. In Ontario, Canada, one school district allows the children to learn and recite poems for parents and friends, uses the Christmas story and songs, and sometimes has a small gift exchange among the children, with candy given by the teacher. In a neighboring district the school has neither a Christmas program nor gift exchange, but they may have a special singing, followed by popcorn and apples for a snack. In one Pennsylvania school the teacher kept Christmas programs from becoming elaborate affairs by requiring that plays be performed without the benefit of a curtain hung to hide "backstage" activity from the observers' view.

Christmas Program a Highlight for Children and Parents

Where Christmas programs are permitted, they are one of the highlights of the school year, especially for the children. The teacher usually spends hours looking for new material not used in previous years, and then copying it by hand from other teachers'

Most Amish schools take very few holidays, preferring to fill the quota of required school days without many breaks. This way they have a longer summer vacation, when children are most needed on the farm.

books and notebooks. (Without electricity, copying machines are not available. Most schools do have access to handcranked duplicating machines with paper masters that can be typed on a manual typewriter or written out by hand.) Pupils work diligently to learn the songs, skits, and poems.

Neighboring schools often schedule their programs on different days so they can visit each other. Parents, small siblings, and friends arrive by foot or buggy, remove their coats, hats, shawls, and bonnets, and pile them on the floor of the porch outside the schoolhouse. (To help them identify which garment belongs to whom, the black shawls and coats are embroidered with elaborately stitched initials in glowing colors. Hats and bonnets often have a piece of paper pinned into them carrying the owner's initials.)

Inside, adults and children alike double up and sit at school desks. The overflow crowd sits on backless wooden benches set up around the room. Often a curtain is hung at the front of the room behind which the children busily prepare for the program. Sheets of paper listing the sequence of events and welcoming everyone to the school lie on desks around the room.

The schoolroom windows are likely decorated with lacy paper cut-out stars, crayon drawings of landscapes and farms, and the blackboard may sport a detailed winter scene done in colorful chalk and headed by a written welcome.

The teacher, who has prepared for this program for many hours, is not seen. The children give the welcome and introduction. The teacher's function is only to prompt and support. In the Pennsylvania schoolhouse program visited by this writer [coauthor Rachel K. Stahl], the students took turns by grades singing and speaking welcomes. The smaller children stepped onto a special little podium at the front of the room to make sure they could be heard and seen when they recited.

Short skits dealt with themes of Christmas: There was the grumpy grandfather. He continually complained about the noise made by the visiting family but was eventually won over by the warm and friendly conversation of the young people, who reminded him of his own younger days. Songs were sung in

When Christmas programs are permitted, they are one of the highlights of the school year for Amish children. Often parents, grandparents, siblings, and even neighboring schools will attend.

unison, with one of the children setting the pitch without a pitchpipe or musical instrument. Familiar carols took on a peculiarly Amish sound when sung in their traditional sliding musical manner.

Since school is where Amish children usually learn the English language, all the poems and songs were done in English, rather than Pennsylvania Dutch. The older grades, however, recited the Christmas story from Luke 2 in High German, which is also taught.

The program drew many smiles and chuckles around the room, but no applause. It lasted for over two hours, with all the material being done from memory. The children used only a few props: candles, a card table, some cut-out paper letters, and a few old hats, coats, and canes.

This writer [coauthor Sara E. Fisher] had one particularly happy Christmas planning and program. The youngest of my three eighth grade girls came to me in November and asked if she and the other eighth grade girls might help plan the Christmas program. I was glad for their help since I do not enjoy planning programs! I gave them my collected materials and a few suggestions and let them do the planning. One play was not suitable for Amish children, so one student rewrote it.

On December 24th, we had our program. All the mothers and most of the fathers came. The teacher of Cherry Lane School came with 22 of her 34 children from that school. The teacher of Meadow View came with 12 of his upper graders. And another teacher came but brought none of her schoolchildren.

The program consisted of 10 poems, six short plays, one exercise, and group singing. It lasted about an hour; then we spent 20 minutes singing the old familiar carols with the audience. Afterwards we all exchanged presents.

Gifts Add to the Celebration

What kinds of gifts do we give? One year we exchanged names to buy each other Christmas presents. The day of the program the gifts were piled on my desk. To start the gift exchange I picked a present from the heap and called out the name. That person came to the front to unwrap the present and show it. Next, that person selected a gift and called out the name on it, and this continued until all the gifts were unwrapped. I had picked the name of one

Some Amish schools have a Christmas exchange. Children and parents sometimes present special gifts such as this quilt to the teacher.

of the eighth-grade girls and gave her a wall hanging of Psalm 23 to embroider and frame. I also bought small gifts for each pupil. For each girl I had a pencil with Christmas greetings on it and stars made from beads which I had purchased from a man crippled with multiple sclerosis. I gave two pens and a pencil to each one of the boys.

Gifts for the Teacher, Too

One of the girls had my name and gave me a macrame plant hanger and a five-pound piece of pre-cooked ham. One of the parents gave me a card with a five dollar bill, and one of them gave four one-pound links of fresh sausage. But after all the gifts were opened, they carried in a blanket chest—the gift from all the parents to the teacher. What a lovely gift to receive! The chest had sentimental value, too, because it was made by a young man from one of my school families who had recently started his own cabinet shop. My gift was his first attempt at making a blanket chest, and a fine job he did! When the children had asked me what I wanted for Christmas, I hinted that I needed a chest to house the presents they had given me other Christmases.

In my third teaching term, they gave me a beautiful quilt with a patch done by each family, representing them in some way. Across the top is a picture of Fairview School done in applique, satin stitch and outline stitch.

Another Christmas they gave me a set of blue bed linens and a blue blanket. One year one family gave me a yellow blanket, while the others gave me a shawl and sweater.

In Lancaster County, several of the one-room schools are shared by Old Order Amish and Mennonites. Some Old Order Mennonites include a meal prepared for the parents after the program, and singing that involves the audience.

Other Programs

This writer made the following entry in a diary from one term of teaching: "The children were making valentines the last few weeks. We had a box from last year which was decorated for Valentine's Day. They put their valentines in there as they finished them or brought them from home. We spent the last period Friday passing out valentines. One family brought puffed rice candy cut in the shape of hearts, one family brought popcorn balls for everyone, and one family passed out valentine candy. I gave each pupil a candy bar and a valentine from a box I had bought."

The Year-End Picnic

Some Old Order Amish schools celebrate the end of the school year with a picnic. Parents bring a picnic lunch of potluck food, they visit, and they watch spirited games of softball and volleyball.

Spontaneous Special Times

Some special times happen apart from traditional holidays. This writer recorded three such events from various terms of teaching.

"Anna Denlinger was a neighbor to Fariview School when I started teaching. I would visit her to get help with problems or just for a shoulder to cry on. She had a school clock hanging in her kitchen, as well as an electric clock. One day I said, 'It's not fair that you have two clocks hanging in your kitchen when there's a

Another special event for an Amish school is the end-of-the-school-year picnic. Parents bring a potluck picnic lunch, they visit, and they watch—or even participate in—softball and volleyball games.

schoolroom nearby that doesn't have any!' She took the hint and asked Jacob Stoltzfus at Pequea Woodworking to make a clock and put it in the schoolroom.

"Jacob didn't say who the clock was from, but we had a pretty good idea. I asked Anna once if she know who gave the clock. She said, 'It's from Santa Claus, isn't it?' I said, 'I think Santa Claus wears a housecoat.' (Anna was wearing a housecoat when I stopped to see her that time.)

"I told the children that we would make a scrapbook for her as a thank you for the clock. On their scrapbook pages they were to write or draw, but not paste. One one side of the page each was to do something about a clock; on the other side they were to do something about school.

"The children did a fine job on the scrapbook, and, when it was finished, I asked Anna to come to school and lead a Spelling Bee and a General Information Quiz. We all enjoyed the Bee and Quiz, and, when we were finished, I said, 'Now the children want to sing a song for you.' Anna started walking toward the back of the room. The children were lined up in front. I asked her not to go back too far so she could hear the words of the song. The children sang this song which I had composed to tell the story of our clock:

Ticktock, ticktock, all day long,
Listen to our school clock's song.
High up on the schoolroom wall,
Telling time for one and all.
Ticktock, Ticktock, all day long,
Listen to our school clock's song.

Ticktock, Ticktock, tell us all,
Who put it up on the wall?
Jacob Stoltzfus came one day,
Put it up and went his way.
Ticktock, Ticktock, one and all,
He put it up on the wall.

Ticktock, Ticktock, please be fair.
Who told him to put it there?
That's a secret he won't say;
We will know it too some day.
Ticktock, Ticktock, now we do—
Anna Denlinger, it was you!

School means hard work, orderliness, and discipline, but it also includes times of fun and celebration for teachers, children, and parents.

"On the morning of my birthday when we were ready to start classes after devotions, I heard someone whistle. I looked up to see who would make such a disturbance, when the tin cans came rolling down the aisles toward the front of the schoolroom. The children had somehow smuggled the cans into their desks as they arrived in the morning without my seeing them. They took the labels off some of the cans so that I wouldn't know what was in them before opening them. The contents varied from baked beans to pears, peaches, plums, apricots, and pineapples."

"Last Friday, just before going home, we exchanged names. Then on Monday, each child brought a lunch for the person whose name she or he drew. The children enjoyed seeing whose lunch they got to eat. At noon on Monday, we washed hands, passed out the lunch boxes as usual, had our prayer, and then I started by giving my lunch to the eighth grade girl whose name I had drawn. She gave hers to the person she packed for, and so on until everyone had someone else's lunch."

Special Schools for Children with Handicaps

There is a lot of close intermarriage within the Amish community. In Lancaster County, the Old Order Amish number 9,000 adult baptized members, so there is a limited pool in which to find a spouse. While it is forbidden to marry one's first cousin, second-cousin marriages are quite common.

Such close marrying can result in children having mental handicaps or children having outstanding intelligence. Another growing problem is that of inherited deafness and dwarfism.

Many Amish communities do not have special schools for their children with handicaps. Often they are simple "dragged along," to quote one teacher, "as best as possible." Others send their children with handicaps to special state-run schools.

A notable exception are two special schools in Lancaster County, Pennsylvania. The project was spearheaded in 1975 by Amish parents whose son was born with hydrocephalus and vision problems. The family spent an enormous amount of labor and love teaching their son the basics of the alphabet. His inability to keep up with his peers in the local one-room school and the teasing he suffered because of it caused him many tears.

1975—The First Special School Opens

This boy was nine when several concerned persons attending the annual school directors' meeting at a local Amish publisher's home discussed at length the problem of teaching special children. It was July 28, 1975 when the idea of a special school for children with handicaps was born.

Money to run the special schools was raised throughout the church districts and came from the Old Order Book Society and the school building fund, which are both supported by parents of school-age children.

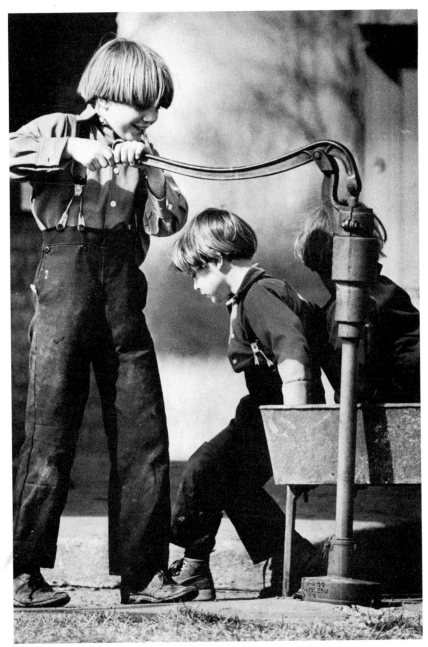

Children are highly valued in the Amish world.

There are two special schools for Amish children with handicaps in Lancaster County, Pennsylvania. Pictured here is Clearview School which, in addition to having regular classes, also houses a classroom for pupils with handicaps.

Many hurdles had to be overcome before the project could actually come to life. Parents and teachers differed about whether these special children should be taught separately or not. The school board had a hard time finding a teacher who would agree to take on the task. A building needed to be found and a car and driver hired to transport these children who lived scattered across the county. And finally, parents needed to be persuaded to enroll their children in the program.

In an effort to find ideas and seek guidance, the Amish school board visited both the special education classes at a public elementary school in the Garden Spot School District in eastern Lancaster County and at the S. June Smith Center, then located in the basement of the Belleview Presbyterian Church in Gap, Pennsylvania. Some Amish children with handicaps were enrolled in these classes at the time.

Finally, on September 15, 1975, Clearview Special School opened with two pupils enrolled. Several weeks later a third pupil joined them. Slowly the school gained acceptance and scholars trickled in. Today there are nine "special students" enrolled at Clearview.

On September 4, 1978, a second special school was opened at Mine Road, Pennsylvania. School enrollment fees were set at $200 per child in 1980. (Parents pay an additional amount if transportation is necessary for their child.) The Old Order Mennonites cooperate with the Old Order Amish in establishing and running the special schools.

Teachers Are Devoted

When this writer [coauthor Rachel K. Stahl] visited Clearview Special School early one winter morning, I was greeted by the teacher who had already been there for over an hour, preparing for the day. She had come early since that was when her ride was available. The second teacher arrived in the car with the children.

On one side of the room, the wall held simple metal hooks for coats, hats, and bonnets. The children's individual places were marked by paper cut-out animals and their names, each lovingly colored. A personalized sense of belonging for each child was evident around the room. Each pupil had a picture of an open mailbox, surrounded by climbing vine flowers and inscribed with their full name, address, and birthday date on the open lid.

As the children arrived and before school began officially, they

The school-day routine at the special schools follows much the same format as at the typical one-room schools. With a much lower teacher-to-student ratio, however, children receive extra attention and encouragement.

had a bit of time to play freely. They threw bean bags, cut out paper dolls, and played with small plastic animals. One of the children with Down's syndrome came over and shook hands, asked who I was, and introduced himself.

Responsibility Is Fostered

When the teacher rang a small handbell, the children put away the games and found their seats. One or two went to the sink and filled their cups with water from the faucets. There was no drainpipe and the overflow from their cups ran into a plastic bucket set underneath the sink. Since this schoolroom is located in the basement of a schoolhouse, and there is no electric pump to pump out the drain, the children covet the responsibility of emptying the bucket when it gets full.

After the children found their seats, the bell was rung again. The teachers stood and took turns reading a passage of Scripture. Then the whole group stood to repeat the Lord's Prayer together. No interpretation of Scripture was given.

In this school the day follows very much the same format as that of other Amish schools. Although none of the children present have gotten beyond a third-grade level of schooling, the teachers make every attempt to teach them reading, writing, and arithmetic. Careful and routine discipline has resulted in a quiet, orderly class. Children who are not reciting or reading to the teacher prepare their lessons for when their turns come. Children who have problems, or are stuck with a word they don't know, raise their hands and wait until the teacher can give them attention.

Adjustments in technique are made for these special children. Flash cards, 10-minute lessons, and individualized instruction help keep them from getting frustrated. One of the children whose attention span was particularly short took periodic breaks from her book to trace cardboard numerals onto a piece of paper and then colored them. A midmorning snack break was unsupervised, and the children ate or played inside and out.

A special long, low table on one side of the room permitted the teacher to sit beside pupils, rather than bending over their desks. The two teachers took turns helping the children, while keeping

Every child is welcomed and accepted into an Amish family and is made to feel like a useful and necessary member of the group.

their eyes on the large group, advising one to study his lesson, another to close her desk, and still another to stay sitting.

Some of these children can barely speak intelligible words. Others forget almost instantly. But they are cared for and are being helped to be as useful as possible in their community. That must be why they appeared so happy.

The special schools are recognized and accepted by the state of Pennsylvania as part of the Amish school system. Teachers receive no special or additional training, since the community feels that experience is the best training.

After the program got rolling, the special schools were inundated by requests from parents who wanted their children with learning handicaps to receive special training. Finally the school boards set guidelines explaining that only children who could not be handled in regular one-room schools would be received into the special schools.

Children who appear to be completely untrainable still attend government-run special education classes, and the Amish community often raises money to donate to such government programs.

The Problems and Joys of Teaching

Twenty-five Amish teachers in nine states and one Canadian province reflected in a survey on the problems and joys of teaching.

New teachers struggle with the recurring comment, "The teacher last year did so-and-so." The teachers that were polled had some suggestions about how to cope with that tension: help the children understand that they are in a new school year with a new teacher who has methods of his/her own. On the other hand, a new teacher should evaluate the practices of the former teacher and look for ways to learn from him or her.

Teaching has many benefits. Meeting former pupils is always a pleasure. In this teacher's [coauthor Sara E. Fisher] opinion, the smiles, firm handshakes, and friendly visits are indeed the greatest and most rewarding and lasting joys teaching has to offer. There are the problems of cheating, lying, and the lack of parental cooperation, but they are minimized when children come to school with a cheery smile and a hearty "Good morning!" and when many parents express their confidence in and pray for the teacher.

When one teacher is responsible for eight grades and all their subjects, there is the problem of doing justice to all the children and all the subjects. A teacher can only hope to create a desire for learning so that the children will pursue the subjects on their own. The important thing in this teacher's view is to mold positive attitudes in each pupil that will be helpful throughout life.

One teacher said, "The children are my greatest joy. To see them come to school filled with happiness and eagerness, and then working with them through difficulties and seeing them open up with mastery of new understandings is like blossoms opening in the spring. What could be more rewarding? This is a little bit of heaven in my hand and in my heart."

One problem new teachers encounter is hearing that "The teacher last year did so-and-so." A new year and a new teacher mean some new methods, but teachers can also learn from what was done in the past.

A teacher can only hope to create a desire for learning so that children will pursue the subjects on their own. The important thing is to mold positive attitudes that last throughout life.

From One Teacher's Diary

"Happiness to a teacher is finding a few mints on her desk with a paper that says, 'From me. Look on other side.' On the other side it said 'Hello!' and the letters, 'L, Y, D, I, A,' were scattered all over the paper.

"It's a pleasure to find at the end of a long list of problems on an arithmetic paper the words, 'I am done. It was fun.' Or finding on a paper that was handed in, the words, 'Hi Teacher! I saw you in church yesterday.'"

A Successful Amish Education: One Amish Teacher's Point of View

But do Amish schools prepare their children for life?

Amish schools prepare their children to be God-fearing, hardworking, and self-supporting persons. They do not, however, teach them to be self-seeking, ambitious, and competitive.

Amish children learn to support themselves by the work of their hands. They learn basic business principles, how to borrow and lend money, how to sew their own clothes, plan and cook meals, prepare a field, and drive a horse and buggy team. Not all of this education happens in the schoolroom, however. The farm and home are seen as viable places for learning also.

An Amish child is taught not to have selfish needs of privacy, space, recognition, admiration, ambition, and rewards that a child in the larger society absorbs as its birthright. At a meeting in Lancaster, Pennsylvania, commemorating the 1972 Supreme Court ruling on the Amish school system, a former Amish man, now with a doctorate in psychology, expressed regrets that he as an Amish child had been born before the Supreme Court ruling. Consequently, his parents were forced to send him to high school where he learned to have social and personal needs that he had never tasted before. His sorrowful conclusion was that it is not possible for most Amish children to go to high school and remain Amish.

An Amish child has an enormous sense of security in community. The practice of mutual aid and caring for one another assures children that they will be supported and kept from complete loneliness, from the time they are born until the time they die. Leaving that security for the fleeting pleasures of higher

Not all education happens in the classroom. The farm and home are seen by the Amish as viable places for learning, explains coauthor Sara E. Fisher.

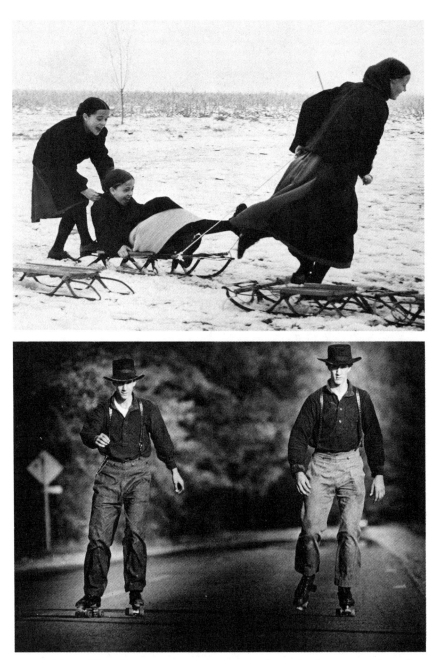

Amish children have an enormous sense of security in community. They know they will be supported, cared for, and kept from complete loneliness as long as they are within that community.

In the end, learning from others, especially those who are older, is central to the Amish way of life.

education is not only risky, but fearsome for most.

If children do leave the Amish community, their skills and ethics are a solid base for making a living. In every community where Amish are settled one can find want-ads in the local paper requesting Amish women to help cook, bake, and clean. The skills of these hardworking people and their conscientious honesty are greatly sought after.

Readings and Sources

Amish Life and History

Good, Merle. **Who Are the Amish?** Good Books, Intercourse, Pennsylvania, 1985.

Good, Merle and Phyllis. **Twenty Most Asked Questions about the Amish and Mennonites.** Good Books, Intercourse, Pennsylvania, 1995.

Hostetler, John A. **Amish Life.** Herald Press, Scottdale, Pennsylvania, 1983.

Hostetler, John A. **Amish Society** (third edition). Johns Hopkins University Press, Baltimore, Maryland, 1980.

Hostetler, John A. and Gertrude E. Huntington. **Amish Children: Education in the Family, School, and Community,** second ed. Harcourt, Brace, Jovanovich College Publishers, New York, New York, 1992.

Hostetler, John A. and Gertrude E. Huntington. **Children in Amish Society.** Holt, Rinehart, and Winston, Inc., New York, New York, 1971.

Kraybill, Donald B. **The Puzzles of Amish Life.** Good Books, Intercourse, Pennsylvania, 1990, 1995.

Mennonite Encyclopedia, The. Herald Press, Scottdale, Pennsylvania, 1959.

Nolt, Steven. **A History of the Amish.** Good Books, Intercourse, Pennsylvania, 1992.

Ruth, John L. **A Quiet and Peaceable Life.** Good Books, Intercourse, Pennsylvania, 1985.

Scott, Stephen. **Plain Buggies.** Good Books, Intercourse, Pennsylvania, 1981.

Scott, Stephen. **Why Do They Dress That Way?** Good Books, Intercourse, Pennsylvania, 1986.

About Amish Schools

Esh, Christian G. **The Beginning and Development of Parochial Special Schools in Lancaster County.** Gordonville Print Shop, Gordonville, Pennsylvania, 1982.

Keim, Albert N. **Compulsory Education and the Amish: The Right Not to be Modern.** Beacon Press, Boston, Massachusetts, 1975.

[Kinsinger, Andrew S.] **Guidelines: In Regards to the Old Order Amish or Mennonite Parochial Schools.** Gordonville Print Shop, Gordonville, Pennsylvania, 1978.

Rodgers, Harrell R., Jr. **Community Conflict, Public Opinion and the Law: The Amish Dispute in Iowa.** Charles E. Merrill Publishing Co., Columbia, Ohio, 1969.

Stoll, Joseph. **Who Shall Educate Our Children?** Pathway Publishing House, Aylmer, Ontario, 1965.

For Amish Teachers and Students

Blackboard Bulletin. Amish periodical published monthly. Pathway Publishing House, Aylmer, Ontario.

Byler, Uria R. **School Bells Ringing: A Manual for Amish Teachers and Parents.** Pathway Publishers, 1969.

Family Life. Amish periodical published monthly. Pathway Publishing House, Aylmer, Ontario

Gordonville Print Shop (Old Order Book Society), Gordonville, Pennsylvania. Publishes a wide variety of materials for Amish schools including reprints of outdated public school materials.

Pathway Reading Series. **First Steps, Days Go By, More Days Go By, Busy Times, More Busy Times, Climbing Higher, New Friends, More New Friends, Building Our Lives, Living Together, Step By Step, Seeking True Values, Our Heritage.** Readers for grades one to eight, especially compiled for Amish schools. Pathway Publishing House, Aylmer, Ontario.

Stoll, Joseph, ed. **The Challenge of the Child: Selections from *The Blackboard Bulletin*, 1957-1966.** Pathway Publishing House, Aylmer, Ontario, 1967.

Teacher Talk: Selections from *The Blackboard Bulletin*, 1968-1972. Pathway Publishing House, Aylmer, Ontario, 1970.

Stories About Amish Children

Beiler, Edna. **Mattie Mae.** Herald Press, Scottdale, Pennsylvania, 1967.

Cousin, Carrie. **Girl in the Mirror.** Pathway Publishing House, Aylmer, Ontario, 1972.

DeAngeli, Marguerite. **Henner's Lydia.** Doubleday, New York, New York, 1937.

DeAngeli, Marguerite. **Yonie Wondernose.** Doubleday, New York, New York, 1944.

Good, Merle. **Amos and Susie: An Amish Story.** Good Books, Intercourse, Pennsylvania, 1993.

Lenski, Lois. **Shoo-Fly Girl.** J. B. Lippincott, Philadelphia, Pennsylvania, 1963.

Moss, P. Buckley and Merle Good. **Reuben and the Blizzard.** Good Books, Intercourse, Pennsylvania, 1995.

Moss, P. Buckley and Merle Good. **Reuben and the Fire.** Good Books, Intercourse, Pennsylvania, 1993.

Naylor, Phyllis R. **An Amish Family.** Lamplight Publishers, New York, New York, 1977.

Pellman, Rachel and Kenneth. **Amish Crib Quilts.** Good Books, Intercourse, Pennsylvania, 1985.

Smucker, Barbara. **Amish Adventure.** Herald Press, Scottdale, Pennsylvania, 1983.

Stoll, Elmo. **The Midnight Test.** Pathway Publishers, Aylmer, Ontario, 1969.

Yoder, Joseph W. **Rosanna of the Amish.** Herald Press, Scottdale, Pennsylvania, 1973.

Index

The Authors

SARA E. FISHER is a member of the Old Order Amish community in eastern Lancaster County, Pennsylvania. She taught eight grades in a one-room Amish school, only stopping in her eighth term because of health reasons.

In the past, Sara helped the Johns Hopkins University Medical School with research among her community and was employed in the kitchen of a local family-style restaurant, as well as holding other jobs. In her retirement, she now does cleaning and also works in a local laundry.

Sara makes her home with her sister Ada; together they cared for their elderly parents for many years, until their deaths. Sara enjoys visiting, reading, and cooking.

RACHEL K. STAHL was born in and grew up in Europe, where her parents spent two decades working under a Mennonite mission board. She has lived most of her adult life in the United States.

Having had most of her schooling in the German language has been very helpful in the research of this book.

Her hobbies are reading, movie-going, and fixing up her house in Lancaster, Pennsylvania.